NATIONAL GEOGRAPHIC
READING EXPEDITIONS®

STAND UP AND SPEAK OUT

The War of the Roses

The Holden Family During the Fight for Woman's Suffrage

By Sarah Glasscock
Illustrated by Margaret Freed

Picture Credits
4 © Bettmann/Corbis; 5 Mapping Specialists, Ltd.;
53 Courtesy of the U.S. Library of Congress;
54 © Bettmann/Corbis; 56 (top) © Peter
Harholdt/Corbis, (left) © Corbis, (right)
Courtesy of the State Historical Society of
Wisconsin Visual Archives

The illustrator gratefully acknowledges the
Wayne County Historical Society of Wooster,
Ohio, for its assistance in the development of
the illustrations.

Produced through the worldwide resources of
the National Geographic Society, John M.
Fahey, Jr., President and Chief Executive
Officer; Gilbert M. Grosvenor, Chairman of the
Board; Nina D. Hoffman, Executive Vice
President and President, Books and Education
Publishing Group.

**Prepared by National Geographic
School Publishing**
Ericka Markman, Senior Vice President and
President, Children's Books and Education
Publishing Group; Steve Mico, Senior Vice
President, Publisher, Editorial Director; Francis
Downey, Executive Editor; Richard Easby,
Editorial Manager; Bea Jackson, Director of
Design; Cindy Olson, Art Director; Margaret
Sidlosky, Director of Illustrations; Matt
Wascavage, Manager of Publishing Services;
Lisa Pergolizzi, Sean Philpotts, Production
Managers, Ted Tucker, Production Specialist.

Manufacturing and Quality Control
Christopher A. Liedel, Chief Financial Officer;
Phillip L. Schlosser, Director; Clifton M. Brown,
Manager.

Editors
Barbara Seeber, Mary Anne Wengel

Book Development
Morrison BookWorks LLC

Book Design
Steven Curtis Design

Art Direction
Dan Banks, Project Design Company

Published by the National Geographic Society
1145 17th Street, N.W.
Washington, D.C. 20036-4688

ISBN: 0-7922-5869-X

2010 2009 2008 2007 2006
1 2 3 4 5 6 7 8 9 10 11 12 13 14 15

๛ Contents ๛

The Fight to Be Heard

The Constitution is a document that outlines the basic rights of American citizens. One example of a basic right is the right to vote, also called suffrage. The Constitution is supposed to protect the rights of all citizens. Yet when it was written in 1787, the document did not include rights for women. As a result, women were not allowed to vote or do many other things that men could do. Some women did not mind. Many others wanted the same rights as men. In particular, they wanted the right to vote. But that meant changing the Constitution. The struggle of women to gain the right to vote came to be known as the woman suffrage movement.

Passing the Nineteenth Amendment

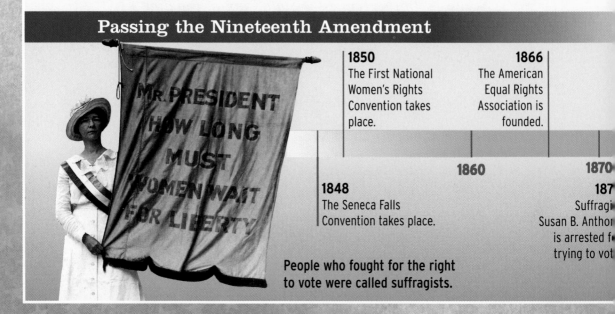

1850
The First National Women's Rights Convention takes place.

1866
The American Equal Rights Association is founded.

1860

1870

1848
The Seneca Falls Convention takes place.

187
Suffragi
Susan B. Anthon
is arrested fo
trying to vot

People who fought for the right to vote were called suffragists.

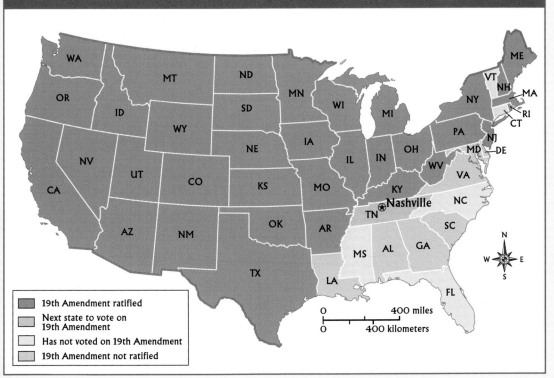

Ratification of the Nineteenth Amendment, 1920

Legend:
- 19th Amendment ratified
- Next state to vote on 19th Amendment
- Has not voted on 19th Amendment
- 19th Amendment not ratified

400 miles
400 kilometers

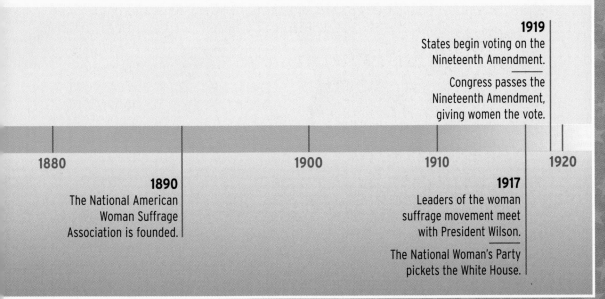

1919
States begin voting on the Nineteenth Amendment.

Congress passes the Nineteenth Amendment, giving women the vote.

1880

1900

1910

1920

1890
The National American Woman Suffrage Association is founded.

1917
Leaders of the woman suffrage movement meet with President Wilson.

The National Woman's Party pickets the White House.

The Holden Family

India Holden

India owns and runs the Holden Dry Goods and Mercantile Store. Her husband, George, used to own the store, but he was killed while fighting in World War I. India is a firm supporter of women's right to vote. India is Susannah and Clay's sister.

Elizabeth Holden

Elizabeth, 12 years old, is India's daughter. She has a lively mind and has been brought up to offer her opinions and ask questions.

Susannah Leonard

Susannah is India and Clay's sister. She is very outspoken and does not support a woman's right to vote. But she is very close to her siblings and niece.

Clay Epperson

Clay is Susannah and India's brother. He lives in Nashville and helps India run the store. Clay believes that women should have the right to vote.

June Granger

June is Clay's girlfriend. They have dated since high school. She does not favor giving women the right to vote. She thinks women should strive to get married and run a household.

FABRIC TOOLS SHOES

Other Characters

Narrator
Salesman
Woman
Male customer
Female customer
Governor Roberts
Representative Banks
Harry Burn
Red Rose Senators 1-2

~ Act I ~

The Setting
Nashville, Tennessee, August 16, 1920

~ ★ ~

Scene 1
In the Holdens' store

Narrator: It is the summer of 1920 in Nashville, the state capital of Tennessee. This summer, the city is buzzing with conversation. In 1919, the United States Congress passed the Nineteenth Amendment, which was the first step towards giving women the right to vote. Next, 36 states have to ratify, or approve, the **amendment** before it can become part of the United States Constitution. Thirty-five states have already done so, and Tennessee is next to vote.

Now, within the week, members of the Tennessee State House must decide whether or not to ratify the Nineteenth Amendment. Everyone knows the vote will be extremely close.

Since the Holden Dry Goods and Mercantile Store is near the state capitol, and India Holden favors

---

amendment – a change to the Constitution

woman suffrage, customers often speak of the amendment and the struggle to pass it. Some customers support the amendment. Others are against it. But India welcomes everyone's comments. As Act I opens, India is stocking the shelves. A salesman enters.

India: May I help you, sir?

Salesman: I'm looking for the owner of this fine establishment. He is about to view some of the most amazing products he's ever seen!

India: I'm India Holden, the owner. What are you selling today?

Salesman: All right, ma'am, you've had your little fun. Is the owner in?

India: I have already told you. I am the owner. What are you selling, sir?

Salesman: Pardon me, ma'am, but this joke has gone on entirely too long. *(Raising his voice)* Come out, come out, wherever you are! I have a case full of time-saving products the women of Nashville will love. Why, these products will be whirring and churning and stirring and flying off your shelves in no time at all! They slice, they dice, they—

(Clay walks up to the counter.)

Salesman: Thank goodness! Why, I was beginning to think your clerk here had locked you in a closet!

Clay: I could hear you shouting from the back of the store. I almost called the police.

India: This salesman would like to speak to the owner of the store, Clay.

Salesman: I'm happy to meet you. You have a fine establishment here. *(Whispering to Clay)* I'd fire that clerk, though, she's got a smart mouth. I wouldn't be surprised if she wasn't a **suffragist.**

Clay: She does believe in the right of women to vote, but I'm afraid I can't fire her. She's my boss. She's the one who owns this store.

(Susannah and Elizabeth enter the store.)

Elizabeth: Mama! Aunt Susannah took me to the hotel for lunch! She taught me how to eat pea soup without slurping! I saw Mrs. Carrie Chapman Catt! I recognized her from her picture in the newspaper, but Aunt Susannah wouldn't let me speak to her.

Susannah: A lady does not make a fool of herself in public. What if people saw you talking to that woman? She should be at home, taking care of her

---

suffragist – a person who is in favor of giving women the right to vote

family. Instead, she's running around the country, telling other people how to lead their lives.

India: *(Teasing)* It's this man's fault. If he weren't selling tools to make women's lives easier, then we'd have to stay home. We'd have too much work to do. I'd better not look at your samples.

Salesman: No, no, no! Women should have these tools to make their lives easier. They should vote! There—I said it! Women should have the right to vote. I don't vote myself because I don't have the time. I—

Susannah: You have the right, and yet you don't use it? Shame on you!

India: Perhaps we should introduce an amendment to take the vote away from men. Perhaps only women should be allowed to vote.

Elizabeth: But that wouldn't be fair! This man may not care, but I bet a lot of other men aren't too lazy to vote!

Salesman: I'm not lazy! I work hard selling my products. Besides, what difference can one vote make?

India: All the difference in the world.

Susannah: If my husband didn't vote, I swear I'd lock him out of the house and tell him to never come home. I may not want to vote myself, but only a coward—or worse, a traitor—would ignore his duty.

Clay: *(Joking)* It's a good thing Horace does exactly what you tell him to do, Susannah.

Salesman: Why, I'm not a traitor! I love my country! I fought in the war! I—

Elizabeth: My father did, too! His name was George Holden. He fought in France. He's buried there.

Salesman: Oh, I'm so sorry. I fought in Germany.

India: Okay, let's see what you're selling. And if you promise to vote, I'll buy some of your goods.

Susannah: And be sure to listen to your wife and your mother when they tell you for whom to vote. Remember that you're voting for them, too.

Salesman: I promise.

(Everyone cheers and claps.)

Scene 2

In the lobby of the Hermitage Hotel

Narrator: The Hermitage Hotel is the headquarters for both pro-suffrage and anti-suffrage groups. *Suffrage* means "the right of voting." Pro-suffragists wear yellow roses. Those who are against suffrage for women wear red roses. For months, people from all over the country have been coming to the Hermitage hotel. They've been trying to persuade the Tennessee **legislators** to vote for, or against, the Nineteenth Amendment.

Tennessee's state **senators** have already voted to ratify the Nineteenth Amendment. On August 13, 25 senators voted for the amendment, and 4 voted against it. In a few days, it will be the **representatives'** turn to vote. Everyone knows this vote will be much closer.

(India, Elizabeth, Susannah, and Clay are in the lobby.)

Elizabeth: Please, Aunt Susannah, come with us. We'll talk to some anti-suffragists, too. Mama says it's good to listen to other people's ideas—especially when they're different from our own.

---

legislator – a member of the U.S. Senate or the House of Representatives
senator – an elected member of the Senate, who votes on policies and laws
representative – an elected member of the House of Representatives, who votes on policies and laws

Susannah: I don't need to listen to anyone else's ideas, thank you very much. I have my own ideas. And one of them is that women and young girls should not be out and about, talking politics. Honestly, India. Come have dinner with Horace and me. You can talk about politics all night long if you'd like.

India: I promised to write letters to the representatives tonight. It's important they understand our views.

Susannah: Well, then let Elizabeth come with me. Wouldn't you like that, Lizzie?

Elizabeth: Oh, no—I'd rather be here. It's exciting! Look, there's June!

(June enters. Elizabeth runs over to greet her.)

India: Susannah, please don't look so upset. You know how much Elizabeth loves you. She didn't mean that she didn't want to be with you.

Susannah: I'm not a child, India. I can understand perfectly well what someone says to me. Good night.

(June and Elizabeth join India and Clay.)

Clay: Is Susannah angry about something?

India: She's disappointed that we're not having dinner with her. How are you, June?

June: Exhausted! I've been talking to Tennessee representatives all day. I've also been trying to pin red roses on them.

India: *(Teasing)* You must tell me what you said, so I can argue against your ideas.

June: I think you know my ideas by now, India. I told the representatives, "Please, don't vote to give me something I don't want."

Elizabeth: Today, I'm going to change your mind, June! What if I want the right to vote? No matter how much I wanted to vote, I couldn't. But if you can vote and you don't want to, then you don't have to.

Clay: That's an excellent point, Lizzie. There's a big difference between having a right and not using it and not having the right at all.

June: Tennessee has already given women the right to vote in presidential elections. Besides, this isn't just about the right to vote. It's also about changing the Constitution, and that could lead to trouble. If you want women to have all the rights that men have, then be prepared. Do you want Elizabeth to have to fight in a war? If she has the same rights that men have, she could be drafted when this country needs soldiers.

Clay: I can't believe you're trying to scare Elizabeth.

Elizabeth: I'm not scared! If I had to fight in a war to help my country, I would. My father did.

India: Besides, giving women the vote will help keep our country out of war. If women have a voice in government, they may be able to steer a more peaceful course.

June: You think that men and women are equal. I've heard you say so. Why, then, would women vote differently than men? Why would our votes bring peace instead of war?

India: There is a difference between having equal rights and having the same opinions. Mothers and wives do not want to see their sons and husbands sent to war.

June: I don't think most sons and husbands want to go to war, either.

Clay: I did. Or I thought I did.

June: Men don't always get to choose whether they fight a war. That's what having the vote has done for them. It has taken away their right to choose.

Clay: Your argument makes no sense, June. How can voting possibly make men have *less* say over the law?

June: I just feel things should stay as they are: Let women rule inside the house and men rule outside it.

Clay: But here you are, June, outside the house. You're even fighting for a cause.

June: I'd rather be at home, waiting for my husband.

Elizabeth: But aren't you and Uncle Clay getting married soon? You can wait for him then.

India: Come on, you two. Shake hands and make up.

Elizabeth: Yes, shake hands! June, show Uncle Clay that you're not as stubborn as he says you are.

India and Clay: Elizabeth!

June: Stubborn? What else does your uncle say about me, Elizabeth?

Elizabeth: That you refuse to listen to anyone else's point of view and—

India: Elizabeth, stop right now. If June wants to know what Clay thinks, she should ask him.

Clay: I was mad at you, June. We'd had that disagreement on Friday. I said some things that I shouldn't have. You know how I feel about you.

June: Thanks to Elizabeth, I do. I may not be able to vote, but I can certainly choose with whom I want to spend my time. Good evening.

Clay: June—wait!

(June leaves, and Clay runs after her.)

Elizabeth: What just happened?

India: June's feelings got hurt.

Elizabeth: But she's wrong!

India: June doesn't think so, Lizzie. She believes what she says just as strongly as you and I do. Telling people they're wrong won't change their minds. You must listen to them. You must really hear what they say.

Elizabeth: Mama—maybe I'm the one who's wrong. I really don't want to fight in a war. I'd just as soon not vote if it meant I had to be a soldier.

India: I don't believe women will have to fight because they win the right to vote. Getting the vote is a tiny step. Saying that women will then have to fight is a huge leap.

Elizabeth: So, you're saying June's wrong, but in a polite way.

India: What I'm saying is that no matter how much you love someone, sometimes it can be very hard to make that person understand you.

(A woman rushes in.)

Woman: India, have you heard? We've gained the support of two more representatives! I'm looking for Harry Burn. Do you know where he is? I'm going to pin a yellow rose on him if it's the last thing I do!

India: Isn't that great news, Lizzie? What's wrong?

Elizabeth: *(Frowning)* I just wish we could convince June to exchange *her* red rose for a yellow one.

Scene 3

In the Holdens' home

Narrator: India is at her desk paying bills for the store, but she can't sit still. She is too excited at the thought that Tennessee might ratify the Nineteenth Amendment. She jumps out of her chair and twirls around the room. India's dance is cut short when she hears someone rattling the front door knob. Quickly, she grabs a broom from the corner and tiptoes toward the door. As the door opens, India raises the broom.

India: I've got a weapon, and I'm not afraid to use it!

(When Susannah enters, India lets the broom drop.)

India: Susannah, I almost hit you with a broom! What are you doing out so late?

Susannah: This is an emergency, India. You're putting your daughter at great risk.

(India turns and walks back into the sitting room. Susannah follows.)

India: By talking to her about women's rights?

Susannah: It's not healthy for a young girl to hear such ideas, especially an impressionable young girl like Elizabeth.

India: Knowing her own mind and speaking out are the greatest lessons I can teach her.

Susannah: Oh, India. Who will ever want to marry Elizabeth if she's so free with her thoughts and ideas?

India: You are free with your thoughts and ideas. And you married a very nice man. Don't you think Elizabeth will find an equal who will value her thoughts and opinions?

Susannah: With my help, she will. I know when to speak and when to hold my tongue. Women are judged not only by what we say, but by how and where we say it. The Hermitage Hotel is no place for my niece to be running about.

India: Then you'd better join us there tomorrow afternoon. You'll do a better job of protecting her if you're near her.

Susannah: I know what you're trying to do, and I'm not going to that hotel. You won't be pinning a yellow rose on me, India Holden.

India: I'm curious: Will you vote for a president this fall? Or will you refuse, because it's not ladylike?

Susannah: What a ridiculous question! Of course I'll vote. I take my responsibilities very seriously. If I have to do something, whether I like it or not, I do it.

India: Then, why not join the fight for woman suffrage? Our country needs your voice.

Susannah: I don't understand it. All of us grew up in the same house, yet you and Clay are so *wrong* about everything. I blame the war.

India: Let's not talk about the war, Susannah. I'm in such a good mood tonight. Here, sit down, and I'll make us some tea.

(Elizabeth sleepily enters the room and sits on a stool inside the door. India and Susannah don't notice her.)

Susannah: You're not listening to me, India. Before you know it, Elizabeth will be going on hunger strikes and getting herself arrested like that suffragist Alice Paul. She'll be marching in the streets, no doubt making a fool of herself.

India: Susannah, don't be so dramatic. Lizzie's a happy and healthy girl.

Susannah: She'll blame you, India, when she's not invited into the homes of the best people. When the finest young men in Tennessee ignore her and no one wants to marry her. When—

India: Many men support the vote for women. A lot of these men have chosen to marry women suffragists. Besides, Elizabeth's only 12 years old!

Susannah: When everyone makes fun of her because of her crazy beliefs, she'll blame you. She'll—

Elizabeth: *(Standing up)* No, I won't! I don't care if people laugh at me! Aunt Susannah, why can't you see how important this is to me?

Susannah: Elizabeth! I didn't realize you were there! I'm only trying to look out for your best interests, dear. You should be enjoying yourself, not parading around with a bunch of . . . of . . . suffragists.

Elizabeth: You say that as if I should be ashamed to be a suffragist. Well, I'm not. I'm proud! And I don't need you to tell me how I should behave!

India: Elizabeth! That's enough! You have strong ideas, but you need to learn how to express them. There is never a cause to be hurtful. Off to your room, Elizabeth. Good night.

Elizabeth: But Mama—

India: Elizabeth, I said good night.

(Elizabeth stares at her mother, and then leaves the room.)

Act II

The Setting

Nashville, Tennessee, August 17, 1920

★

Scene 1

In Elizabeth's bedroom

Narrator: Elizabeth wakes up tired and grumpy. After Susannah's visit, she tossed and turned in bed all night long. Now she sits in front of her window, working on a scrapbook about the Nineteenth Amendment. She has newspaper articles, sketches she's made of the people she's met, and pressed roses, both yellow and red. As she works, she thinks about her aunt. She doesn't understand how Susannah and June can be against the idea of women voting. Elizabeth begins to wonder if she and her mother are wrong for wanting all American women to have the right to vote. During this scene, Elizabeth thinks out loud. As she thinks about the opinions of her mother, Clay, Susannah, and June, each character steps in to speak his or her part.

Elizabeth: Everybody can't be right. If we all have different ideas about the same thing, then somebody has to be wrong. Clay, Mama, and I believe that women should have the right to vote. Aunt Susannah and June don't. They must be wrong. But if they're wrong, why can't they see it? This is making my head hurt. Okay, Elizabeth, think hard now. What would Mama say about this?

(India enters.)

India: During the war, many women worked hard. We ran family businesses and worked in factories. We stepped in when the men went to war. Some of them didn't come home. So we still work hard. Some of us learned that we enjoy working. We wouldn't give it up even if we could. What started the American Revolution? Taxation without representation! And now, over a hundred years later, I pay taxes, yet I'm still not allowed to vote for the people who represent me in this country.

Elizabeth: Okay, since women run businesses and pay taxes, then they should have a voice in government. I know what Aunt Susannah would say about that.

(Susannah enters.)

Susannah: Just last year, didn't the Tennessee State House say that the women of this state could vote in presidential elections? And the people in Washington, D.C., already have too much power. I believe the people of Tennessee, not Washington, should be deciding our future.

Elizabeth: That makes sense to me. What would Mama say about it?

India: Every American woman should have the right to vote in all elections—no matter what state she lives in. Women in some states still can't vote in *any* election. And without a constitutional amendment, a state can take the vote away from women. Did you know certain women in the American colonies had the right to vote? After the American Revolution, no women had that right.

Elizabeth: Look how hard we're fighting to get the Nineteenth Amendment passed. People can't just add an idea to the Constitution. You've got to make sure most Americans agree with it. It's really hard to change the Constitution. If the Nineteenth Amendment passes, it'll pass because most Americans want women to vote. But that's not what June would say.

(June enters.)

June: Susannah's right. If this amendment passes, then Washington will be able to tell women what to do. If we're equal to men, then we'll have to fight in wars. We might be forced to go to work. Women will *lose* their right to be protected.

Elizabeth: Is that true? Uncle Clay, what would you say?

(Clay enters.)

Clay: In some states, women have been able to vote for the president since the last century. Other states still deny women that right. How can we truly elect a president when women in Wyoming can vote, but women in Kentucky can't? This country has to take a stand. It has to say loudly and clearly that all American women deserve the right to vote. And June, my love, no one could force you to do anything.

June: You live in dreams, Clay. You think giving women the vote will make this country better. You don't see the danger. You refuse to see how it will change everything. I don't want to be equal to a man. I don't want your problems.

Elizabeth: *(Clapping her hands)* Okay, that's enough!

(The other characters leave. India knocks and enters.)

India: I thought I heard you shouting.

Elizabeth: I don't feel well today.

India: Are you worrying about what Aunt Susannah said last night? You know how much she loves you. She would never want to hurt you.

Elizabeth: Well, she did.

India: I know this is hard, Lizzie. But even people who care about each other often have different ideas about things that are important to them.

Elizabeth: What if Tennessee says yes? What if women get the right to vote, but Aunt Susannah and June won't speak to us anymore? If I had to choose between giving up the vote or giving up family and friends, I don't know what I'd do.

India: Let me ask you this: If Tennessee says no to the Nineteenth Amendment, will you stop speaking to Aunt Susannah and June?

Elizabeth: No, but I hope they wouldn't act too happy about it when I was with them.

India: People don't always agree with each other. That's what makes life interesting.

Elizabeth: Right now, life seems *too* interesting.

India: I'm sorry, sweetie. I shouldn't have put you in the middle of this fight. You shouldn't be so worried about how Tennessee votes.

Elizabeth: Mama, if Dad were still alive, what side would he be on? Would you and he be fighting about the vote for women?

India: He'd be for the amendment. But I think he'd tell me to let you enjoy the summer. He'd say there should be no more talk about voting today.

Scene 2

In the Holdens' store

Male Customer: Tomorrow's the big day, Mrs. Holden. I suppose you and Clay are going to the capitol.

India: I wouldn't miss it—no matter what happens. It's going to be an historic day.

Female Customer: Suppose I need some cake flour tomorrow, India. If you close the store, how am I expected to get my chores done? I say, this vote thing has turned Nashville upside down.

India: No need to worry, Mr. and Mrs. Jenkins will be running the store tomorrow in my place.

Male Customer: All this hubbub is good for the city. It brings in more money, and once people visit Nashville, they'll want to come back.

Female Customer: Don't tell me you approve of what's going on at the Hermitage Hotel, sir! Red roses, yellow roses, everyone in an uproar—

Clay: *(Laughing)* It's not that bad.

Female Customer: I don't see what you've got to laugh about, Clay Epperson. I happen to know that you and June called it quits yesterday afternoon, quite loudly, in the middle of the hotel lobby.

India: Is that true, Clay?

Clay: We've both decided to think about things. We'll decide what happens after the vote tomorrow.

Female Customer: Well, it's quite clear, Mr. Epperson, how you stand on the issue. You are both losing something because of your views.

Male Customer: Here's my advice to you, Clay: Hold on to June. A little arguing is good for a marriage. Once, my wife didn't speak to me for a whole year.

Clay: What did you fight about?

Male Customer: I can't remember. Say, do you have any peppermint candy?

Clay: How did you and your wife make up?

Male Customer: One day, she just started talking to me again. I was mighty happy. I'll tell you what—go talk to that girlfriend of yours.

Female Customer: You mean talk her out of her ideas.

(Susannah enters, wearing a red rose.)

Susannah: *(Loudly)* Ladies and gentlemen, don't take your business elsewhere! Not everybody in this family supports the vote for women. Someone in this family shares your ideas!

India: Susannah, what are you doing?

Susannah: *(In a hushed tone)* I know you're losing customers right and left because of your pro-voting views. I am bringing balance back to your business. *(Loudly again)* So, ladies and gentlemen, don't close out your accounts in this great store!

Female Customer: What did I tell you? Every time you turn around, someone's waving a rose in your face and telling you what to think! This is too much!

(She leaves.)

Susannah: India, I've warned you and Clay time and time again about bringing politics into the store.

India: You're the only one wearing a rose in here.

Susannah: Your views are so well-known that you might as well be covered in yellow roses.

Male Customer: I'll be back later for those peppermints.

(He hurries out.)

Clay: Good work, Susannah. You just drove away two customers.

Susannah: You'll thank me, once all this silliness is over.

Clay: I don't think we will.

Susannah: You can stand up and speak out all you want. But if I have a different view, I have to hold my tongue!

India: Why are you wearing a red rose all of a sudden?

Susannah: If you must know, I was feeling left out. Everyone in town seems to be on one side or the other. How will I be able to celebrate tomorrow, or exclaim bitterly, if no one knows where I stand?

Clay: Everyone in Nashville knows where you stand.

Susannah: I never told you and India, but because of you and your opinions, I've lost two friends. No matter how much I protested, they said I must be in favor of the vote for women. Not to mention how you've dragged Elizabeth into this mess.

(Elizabeth leads June into the store.)

Elizabeth: Uncle Clay, look who I found! June!

(Elizabeth stops, shocked, when she sees the red rose pinned to her aunt's dress.)

Elizabeth: Aunt Susannah! Don't you love us at all?

Susannah: *(Surprised)* Of course, I do! I'm wearing this red rose for your sakes.

June: You should be wearing it for your own sake.

Clay: June, I'm so glad to see you. I'm sorry about the things I said yesterday. I'm the one who's stubborn, not you.

June: No. I'm more stubborn than you are.

Clay: I don't want to argue, but I'm much more stubborn.

June: No, I'm worse than a mule. Once I've made up my mind, you can't drag me away from an idea.

Susannah: You're both stubborn. Let's move on.

(June and Clay talk softly to each other.)

(The male customer rushes in.)

Male Customer: Have you heard? Some of the representatives want to stop the vote tomorrow! They're planning to sneak out of the state at midnight!

Susannah: Those pro-vote people will stop at nothing!

Male Customer: It's the anti-vote people who don't want to face their responsibilities!

Susannah: I don't believe it! Only cowards would run like that.

Elizabeth: Mama, why would they leave?

India: If there aren't enough representatives on the floor of the capitol tomorrow, then the amendment can't be voted on.

Susannah: They'll have to come home sooner or later— and I'll be waiting to give them a piece of my mind! And to think I told Horace to vote for some of those men.

India: If the amendment passes tomorrow, you can vote them out of office yourself.

Susannah: *(Pulling off the rose and throwing it on the ground)* I refuse to support anything those ridiculous politicians support. I'm changing sides!

༄ Act III ༄

The Setting

Nashville, Tennessee, August 18, 1920

༄ ★ ༄

Scene 1

In the Tennessee State Capitol Building

Narrator: The day of the vote on the Nineteenth Amendment has finally arrived. It's a hot and humid summer day. People furiously fan themselves and talk about how the vote will go. India, Elizabeth, and Clay, all wearing yellow roses, sit together. June is sitting in front of them, wearing a red rose.

Last night, a group of Tennessee representatives tried to leave the state to stall the vote. But the United States Supreme Court said that they must return and do their jobs. India and the other suffragists know the amendment is in trouble and may not pass. After all the months of writing letters and talking to legislators, the amendment may be defeated by only two votes. If Tennessee doesn't ratify it today, the Nineteenth Amendment will most likely never become part of the Constitution. The state's 96 representatives are seated on the main floor. The second-floor gallery of seats is packed with pro- and anti-suffragists, wearing yellow and red roses.

Everyone waits for Governor A. H. Roberts to arrive and begin the vote.

India: ... 42, 43, 44, 45, 46, 47. I must have counted wrong. Surely more of the representatives are wearing yellow roses than red roses!

Elizabeth: June's waving at us.

(June holds up two fingers and then points at her red rose.)

Clay: It looks like she's counted 49 to 47, too.

Elizabeth: Do you think Aunt Susannah's going to come? She was so angry yesterday.

India: She'll be glad the Supreme Court told the representatives to get back here. Even if the amendment doesn't pass today, I'll bet she works hard to make sure none of those men get re-elected.

Clay: There's Governor Roberts. The representatives can start voting now!

India: The moment has finally arrived!

(As the governor walks in, Susannah enters the second floor.)

Elizabeth: It's Aunt Susannah! I can't tell if she's wearing a rose or not.

(Susannah sits beside Clay.)

Susannah: *(Fanning herself)* Why in the world do they do these things in the summer? Everyone is simply wilting in the heat.

Elizabeth: It's 49 red roses to 47 yellow roses.

India: We still have a chance. Someone might have a change of heart.

Susannah: At least the cowards decided to show up.

Governor Roberts: By my authority as the governor of this fair state, I bring this meeting of the Tennessee House of Representatives to order! You are here today to ratify the Nineteenth Amendment to the United States Constitution, or not. The Senate has voted for ratification. Gentlemen, it is now up to you!

Red Rose Senator 1: I move that we table the vote.

(People boo from the second floor.)

Red Rose Senator 1: I don't believe we've had enough time to discuss what this amendment will mean to our country and its people.

Red Rose Senator 2: I second the motion!

Susannah: Cowards! Stop dilly-dallying and vote on the amendment!

Narrator: The representatives vote quickly on the motion to table, or delay, the vote. The motion is defeated. The vote will go on. One by one, the men say yes or no to the Nineteenth Amendment.

Governor Roberts: Representative Banks Turner, how do you vote?

India: We are at 47. They have 48.

Elizabeth: Come on, Mr. Banks, vote for us!

Susannah: I don't think he will. He's wearing a red rose.

Representative Banks: This has been a great and difficult decision for us all. I must, however, cast my vote for ... RATIFICATION!

(There are cheers and boos. India, Clay, Elizabeth, and Susannah stand up and clap.)

India: It's a tie! We've still got a chance!

Susannah: Turner Banks, you are a hero!

Elizabeth: What happens now?

India: They vote again to see if they can break the tie.

Governor Roberts: *(Pounding a gavel)* Order! Quiet!

Narrator: As the crowd settles down, the representatives cast their votes a second time.

Clay: Now, there are 48 for, and 47 against. It looks like it's going to be another tie.

Governor Roberts: Representative Harry Burn, how do you vote?

Harry Burn: *(Clearing his throat and thrusting his hands into his jacket pocket)* Against.

Governor Roberts: Speak up!

Harry Burn: *(Louder)* Against.

Governor Roberts: We have another tie. Let me say this: No one is going home until we break the tie. So search your souls, gentlemen, and do what you must!

Narrator: The third vote begins. The heat in the capitol is almost unbearable.

Elizabeth: I can't stand much more of this!

India: Someone has to change his mind. No one can leave until the tie is broken.

Clay: Yes, but who? And to which side will he go?

Susannah: Thank goodness, Turner Banks is sticking to his yes vote. I like a man who does his duty and stands up for what he believes in.

Narrator: Then, only one representative is left. The vote is 47 against ratification and 48 for ratification.

India: Harry Burn, pull off that red rose!

Susannah: He's not going to change his mind, India. Look at him. He's just a boy.

Clay: He's the youngest representative we've got.

Elizabeth: Just because you're young doesn't mean you don't have any courage! Come on, Harry Burn! Vote yes! I know you can do it!

Governor Roberts: Representative Harry Burn of McMinn County, Tennessee, how do you vote?

(Burn pulls a piece of paper out of his pocket and stares at it.)

Governor Roberts: Harry Burn how do you vote?

Harry Burn: *(Softly)* I vote . . . I vote . . . yes.

India: *(Jumping to her feet)* That's it! 49 to 47! We've done it!

(Some people groan, while others react with disbelief and joy.)

Governor Roberts: *(Pounding his gavel)* The great state of Tennessee has ratified the Nineteenth Amendment to the United States Constitution by a vote of 49 to 47!

Elizabeth: Oh, no! What are they doing to poor
Harry Burn?

Narrator: A group of angry representatives chases Burn.
He climbs out a window to escape. The piece of paper
he was holding flutters to the ground.

Susannah: Cowards! Leave that man alone! Leave him
alone, I say!

Clay: I'd better go down and see if I can help.

(He rushes out just as June approaches.)

June: Congratulations, India. It was a hard-won fight.

India: *(Hugging June)* I hope you'll be able to see it as your victory, too.

Elizabeth: Uncle Clay wasn't running away from you, June. He had to go save poor Harry Burn.

Susannah: Whatever made that young man change his mind, I wonder?

Scene 2

In the Holdens' store

Narrator: It is later in the day, the same day as the vote. Happy and relieved that the long fight is over, India, Elizabeth, and Susannah return to the store.

Elizabeth: Aunt Susannah, are you really glad about what happened today? I hope you can see how wonderful this is, to finally have the vote!

Susannah: Indeed I do. I can't wait to cast my vote and turn those cowards out of office! It's shameful, the way they behaved!

India: Leaving the state would have been one way to stop the vote. It might have given the anti-suffragists time to win more representatives to their side.

Susannah: Thats no excuse. What if President Wilson tried to leave the country when he had to make a difficult decision? What if Clay had tried to run away, instead of fighting for his country? It's shameful! Look at Harry Burn and what he did today!

India: Poor Harry Burn. I'm not sure he's feeling like a hero right now. But he is a hero. He was under a lot of pressure, but he finally took the right course. Harry Burn, we thank you!

Elizabeth: Why do you think he changed his mind? It was awfully strange how he went back and forth.

Susannah: We'll ask your Uncle Clay when he comes back from rescuing the poor boy. But right now, we'd better start planning his wedding to June.

Elizabeth: His wedding? I know they're engaged, but are they really getting married so soon?

Susannah: Of course they are. Now, India, you and I would look lovely in peach satin. Why don't you order two or three bolts of it?

India: Peach certainly is your color, Susannah. But perhaps we should wait until—

Susannah: Nonsense! Now, I know Mrs. Dudley will want to throw a little party for June, so I had better call her this week. She's a very busy woman.

Elizabeth: Do you think June will ask me to be in the wedding? I'm too old to be a flower girl, and too young to be a bridesmaid. But I would love to wear a pretty dress and walk down the aisle!

India: Both of you calm down. I think you're getting ahead of yourselves. When June and Clay get married, they'll make their own wedding plans.

Susannah: Just because we've won the right to vote doesn't mean we have to stop planning weddings. You yourself said it's all about having a choice. Well, I choose to help plan their wedding. They're going to need somebody to tell them what to do.

India: You are very good at telling people what to do. But sometimes, Susannah, . . . sometimes . . .

Elizabeth: Sometimes, Aunt Susannah, what you say hurts people's feelings.

Susannah: Why, Elizabeth, what do you mean? A lady never hurts people's feelings.

Elizabeth: You hurt my feelings. You told Mama that no one would ever want to marry me. But I think someday someone will love me because of my ideas.

Susannah: Of course they will, Lizzie! Just remember: You'll catch more flies with honey than with vinegar. That's what my mother used to say.

Elizabeth: Aunt Susannah, I don't think you're listening to me. You really did hurt my feelings.

Susannah: Oh, Lizzie, I am sorry. How can I make it up to you?

Elizabeth: You already did—by changing your mind about the vote for women. Mama, does this mean that I can run for president some day?

India: I don't see why not. I'd vote for you.

Susannah: Honestly, India! Women voting is one thing, but women running for office is another!

(Clay enters. His clothes are dirty.)

Susannah: Clay, look at you! Your clothes are filthy. You look like you've been in a tussle.

India: I hope Harry Burn looks better than you do, Clay. What happened?

Elizabeth: Where's June?

Susannah: Yes, Clay, where is June? I have a list of things to talk to her about. Flowers, the cake, her dress, our dresses—

Clay: June's going home.

Susannah: Of course, she'll want to talk to her mother about the wedding plans, but I do think—

India: Susannah, stop talking for a minute. Let Clay catch his breath.

Clay: June and I aren't getting married. She says she couldn't stand being on the opposite side of a fight with me again. But the real truth is that she thinks we have different ideas about how we want to live our lives.

Susannah: Nonsense! Everyone's tired and saying all sorts of silly things. We all just need a good night's rest, you'll see.

India: Please, Susannah. Clay is not a boy. Let him speak about this freely.

Clay: Some couples can do it, I guess. They have different ideas and get along. For some reason, June and I can't. We just think too differently about things. We love each other, but we know we wouldn't be able to live together.

India: Oh, Clay, I'm so sorry. I admire June so much. She is such an honest, decent person.

Susannah: Do you know who I really admire? Mrs. Dudley's daughter, Iris. She was sitting behind us. She's a lovely girl, Clay. I think you and she might really—

India, Elizabeth, and Clay: (*In unison*) Susannah, stop!

Narrator: What made Harry Burn change his vote that day? The answer is in the piece of paper he dropped on the floor. It was a telegram from his mother. She wrote:

"Dear Son: Hurrah and vote for suffrage! Don't keep them in doubt! I noticed some of the speeches against. They were bitter. I have been watching to see how you stood, but have not noticed anything yet. Don't forget to be a good boy and help Mrs. Catt put the 'rat' in ratification. Signed, Your Mother."

The next day, Harry Burn explained his change of heart. "I want to take this opportunity to state that I changed my vote in favor of ratification because, one, I believe in full suffrage as a right, two, I believe we had a moral and legal right to ratify, and three, I know that a mother's advice is always safest for her boy to follow, and my mother wanted me to vote for ratification."

So, you see, one person can make a difference. Mrs. Burn's words changed her son's mind. And his vote changed the history of our country. The Nineteenth Amendment was ratified. Women in the United States could no longer be denied the right to vote.

Woman Suffrage in America

The Leaders

Women's struggle to win voting rights started long before 1920. The first public meeting for woman suffrage was held in 1848 in Seneca Falls, New York. In the years that followed, many women started speaking out in defense of their rights. In 1866, suffragists Susan B. Anthony, Elizabeth Cady Stanton, and Lucretia Mott formed the

Suffragist leaders Alice Paul, Sue White, Florence Boeckel, Mary Winsor, Anita Pollitzer, Sophie Meredith, and Evelyn Wainwright

American Equal Rights Association. This organization included men and women, whites and African Americans. Their goal was to gain suffrage for *all* American citizens. Other suffragists such as Alice Paul and Lucy Stone also helped fight for women's right to vote.

Changing Minds

By the late 1800s, American women had gained many rights. They could work outside of the home. They could own their own property. They could even go to college. But women in

America could not vote. When World War I started, many men left home to fight in Europe. With no men to run factories and businesses, women were asked to take over. Women worked hard to make supplies needed for the war. They also took care of their families by themselves. By the time the war ended, women had proved that they could do the same work as men.

These women took men's factory jobs during World War I.

The Nineteenth Amendment

In 1918, President Woodrow Wilson said in a speech, "We have made partners of women in this war. Shall we admit them only to a partnership of suffering and sacrifice and toil, and not to a partnership of right?" Within a year, Congress passed the Nineteenth Amendment, giving women the right to vote. Thirty-six states had

Women celebrate after hearing that the Nineteenth Amendment has been ratified.

to approve, or ratify, the amendment for it to become a law. One by one, the states voted. On August 18, 1920, Tennessee became the 36th state to approve the amendment. American women had finally won the right to vote.

Write a Newspaper Article

Imagine the year is 1920. You are a newspaper reporter assigned to profile a family with mixed views on women's right to vote. You have chosen to profile the Holden family.

- Copy the chart shown below into your notebook.
- In the left column, list three historical events discussed in the story or the time line in the order they occurred.
- In the second column, list information about each event.
- Use the information from the story and other resources to complete your chart.
- Then write your article. Use dates and clue words such as *first, next, then,* and *last* to show the sequence of the events.

Event	Information about the event
1. In 1919, Congress passed the Nineteenth Amendment.	• This was the first step in giving women the right to vote. India supports the vote.
2.	
3.	

Read More About the Suffrage Movement

Find and read more books about the Suffrage Movement. As you read, think about these questions. They will help you understand more about this topic.

- Why is it so important that all people have the right to vote?

- Why did some women not want the right to vote?

- What did men do to help women gain their voting rights?

- Why do Americans vote every two years instead of keeping representatives and officials for life?

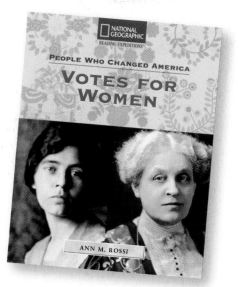

SUGGESTED READING
Reading Expeditions
People Who Changed America: Votes for Women